GLORIA ESTEFAN

GLORIA ESTEFAN

Pop Sensation
by Leslie Gourse

A Book Report Biography
FRANKLIN WATTS
A Division of Grolier Publishing
New York / London / Hong Kong / Sydney
Danbury, Connecticut

Cover illustration by Joan M. Toro, interpreted from a photograph
by © Liaison Agency, Inc./Evan Agostini

Photographs ©: AP/Wide World Photos: 84 (Mark Foley), 93
(Clark Jones/Sears), 69 (Mark Lennihan), 73 (Stuart Ramson), 49
(Amy Sancetta), 17, 44; Archive Photos: 31 (Esteban Bucat/Newsphotos),
92 (Jeff Christensen/Reuters); Corbis-Bettmann: 25, 75 (Reuters), 29
(UPI); Globe Photos: 15 (D. Parker/Alpha London); Liaison Agency, Inc.:
53 (E. Sander), 57 (Richard Vogel); Miami Herald Publishing Co: 67
(Al Diaz); Retna Ltd./Camera Press Ltd.: 34 (Freek Arriens), 95
(George Bodnar), 10 (Gary Gershoff), 77 (Steve Granitz), 19
(Scott Weiner); The Palm Beach Post/Post Stock: 66 (Allen Eyestone).

Visit Franklin Watts on the Internet
at:
http://publishing.grolier.com

Library of Congress Cataloging-in-Publication Data

Gourse, Leslie
Gloria Estefan : pop sensation / Leslie Gourse.
    p. cm.—(A book report biography)
Includes bibliographical references and indexes.
Discography: p.
Videography: p.
Summary: Presents a biography of the Cuban-born singer and
composer.
ISBN 0-531-11569-0 (lib. bdg.)   0-531-16457-8 (pbk.)
    1. Estefan, Gloria—Juvenile literature. 2. Singers—United States—
Biography—Juvenile literature. [1. Estefan, Gloria. 2. Singers. 3. Cuban
Americans—Biography. 4. Women—Biography.] I. Title. II. Series.
ML3930.E85 G68 2000

                                                    00-020835

CONTENTS

GLORIA ESTEFAN

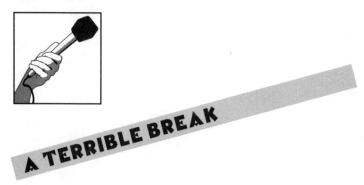

CHAPTER ONE

A TERRIBLE BREAK

A petite, dark-haired singer with shining eyes, Gloria Estefan rose to stardom in the 1980s with her English and Spanish pop hits. Being Cuban-born, Estefan produced Spanish-language hits first. Estefan was born Gloria María Fajardo in Havana and moved to Miami, Florida, with her political refugee family in the early 1960s.

Estefan's professional career began in 1975. Under the guidance of her husband and manager, Emilio Estefan, Gloria Estefan became lead singer of the Miami Sound Machine, a group Emilio had helped to found. By the early 1980s, Gloria Estefan was writing some of the group's songs. Then, when the Miami Sound Machine scored two big hits, "Dr. Beat," and "Conga," Estefan began to cross over to the English-language pop charts. No matter what she sang—mellow ballads or uptempo, exciting songs—she and the

Gloria Estefan rose to stardom in the 1980s as singer for the Miami Sound Machine.

Miami Sound Machine, adept at playing Latin and American rhythms, charmed the public.

By the late 1980s, having traveled constantly, particularly in South America, Asia, and Europe, Gloria had become a star. The group had successfully crossed over to become a mainstream American pop group, supported by infectious Latin rhythms. Emilio Estefan, recognizing his wife's appeal, changed the name of the group to Gloria Estefan and the Miami Sound Machine. Emilio had a great talent for promoting the group and his wife. He coordinated all aspects of the group's touring schedule, compositions, arrangements, band members, and business deals for shows and recording contracts. He made doors open.

It seemed as though the Estefans were leading charmed lives. But on March 20, 1990, something terrible happened that Emilio could not plan for or control. And it nearly robbed them of everything they had achieved. In the morning, the Estefans' tour bus departed from New York City for Syracuse; at the same time, a truck driver named Heraldo Samuels climbed into the cab of a large truck in Newark, New Jersey, loaded with nineteen tons of pitted dates from the Middle East. By ten o'clock, he was on the road and headed for Toronto, Canada.

About an hour after the Estefans' bus left New York, Gloria, who always found it easy to fall asleep, became drowsy while watching a movie. Her bus headed west on Route 80 through New Jersey, rolling along toward Pennsylvania. Behind them somewhere was the truck driven by Heraldo Samuels. There may have already been some patches of ice or slippery spots on the road. And it began to snow.

Ahead of the Estefan bus, one truck driver had an accident. Because of snow or slush on the road, his truck jackknifed and blocked all westbound traffic on Interstate 380. Another truck driver saw the problem and stopped. So did other cars and trucks. The driver of Gloria's bus slowed down and came to a full stop in the line of traffic. Gloria felt the bus stop and woke up from her nap.

But one truck behind her wasn't stopping. It actually seemed to be gaining speed as it approached the stalled traffic. Other people in the traffic jam watched in horror as that truck, seemingly unable to stop, slammed into the back of the big tour bus carrying the Estefans. Pushed forward, Gloria's bus hit the truck in front of it. There was a crashing of metal and shattering of glass. Then every thing fell silent. And the snow kept falling.

Gloria heard an explosion, she later said. Her body was flung from the couch onto the floor of the bus. The bus driver was hurt, and Emilio was knocked out of his sneakers. He ran to see how

Gloria and their son were faring. Finding Gloria on the floor, Emilio asked, "Baby, are you all right?"

She said, "I think I broke my back."

Emilio was frightened and told her that she must have strained it in some way. But she sensed the truth. Gloria told him, "Go check the baby." She lay on the floor "for what seemed like forever when I heard Emilio crying," she recalled. "What's happened to Nayib? I thought. If Nayib was badly injured, or worse, my life was over."

She said, "I think I broke my back."

Emilio found Nayib under some debris. His shoulder was hurting, but it turned out that he had only broken his collarbone. And he wasn't crying. When Gloria saw him with Emilio, she said, "I knew I could manage whatever else might happen."

But Estefan had no idea how difficult and painful her recovery would be. But the difficult days of her childhood, as an impoverished refugee from the Cuban revolution, had prepared her for the struggle. Nothing had been easy in Gloria Estefan's life until she was a grown woman.

In the years just before the accident, she had earned so much success, and she was such a busy star, that her difficult childhood may have been little more than a dim memory. In 1987, Gloria and the group began a world tour that lasted twenty-two months. It kept her away from Emilio and their son Nayib in their home base of Miami Beach for months at a time.

Her fame mounted throughout the late 1980s. In 1988, the Miami Sound Machine had been named best pop/rock group at the American Music Awards. In 1989, several songs from her "Cuts Both Ways" album made the top ten of the pop music charts. And she also won the Songwriter of the Year Award from Broadcast Music Inc. (BMI), the agency that controls and sells the rights to songs performed by artists other that the actual composers. Estefan was also nominated for a Grammy that year, as was Emilio—for producer of the year. Neither Estefan won, but CBS, their record label, honored them with a Crystal Globe Award, which is given to artists who sell millions of albums outside the United States.

In 1989, Estefan went on a shorter tour, this time with Emilio, Nayib, Nayib's tutor, and a full staff for the group. In Europe, the shows were sold out. Nayib was fascinated by the backstage life of his pop-star mom. On the road, he had to study with his tutor to keep up with his studies for school back home in Miami. But he was leading a storybook existence that other kids could only

The Estefans, Emilio, Gloria, and son Nayib, pose here in 1991, all fully recovered from the bus accident that nearly ruined their lives.

dream about. Then the group returned to the United States and performed in the Midwest.

The constant traveling took its toll on Gloria. She caught the flu, and she pushed her voice so much that she damaged some blood vessels in her throat. In December, the family went back to their home in the exclusive enclave of Star Island, situated in Miami's Biscayne Bay. Gloria needed rest.

Young and strong, she recovered by January 1990 and resumed her tour. Adding to her energy level was her happiness at her highly successful career. She had accomplished the nearly impossible: She had become a star in both the Latin and English-speaking pop charts. And the Spanish-speaking audience in the United States kept increasing. By 1990, there were more than twenty million people of Hispanic background, nearly 10 percent of the U.S. population.

One of the tour's most successful shows was performed at Madison Square Garden in New York City. As Estefan told an interviewer, she was wife and mother, but for the few hours she was on stage, she belonged totally to the people in front of her. The crowd at the show rose to their feet and danced as she sang hits such as "Conga" and "Get on Your Feet."

After the New York show and another in Philadelphia, the Estefans were invited to Washington, D.C., to meet with then-President George

In March 1990, the Estefans met with then-President George Bush to receive an award for their work on his antidrug campaign.

Bush. Gloria received an award for an antidrug campaign that she was involved with. It was a great honor for Gloria, who had left Cuba with little more than the clothes on her back. After the ceremony, the Estefans and their staff boarded a rented tour bus back to New York. During the five-hour trip, most of the group slept, and upon reaching New York, the Estefans had dinner with a friend, Spanish singer Julio Iglesias. The next morning, the Estefans began their ill-fated trip to Syracuse.

Before the accident, and while Gloria Estefan slept, Emilio was busy on his cellular phone, conducting business. He was the force behind the success of the Miami Sound Machine, and he was always on the job. His ideas and coaching had pushed the group forward and had nurtured Gloria through her days as a plump teenager to her reign as a trim, glamorous international star.

Gloria and Emilio Estefan are exact opposites who complement each other perfectly, as Gloria once told a reporter. Emilio "has a lot of drive, and I'm a couch potato," she said. He "pushed me along and motivated me with a lot of things, and at the same time I keep him from having a nervous breakdown."[1] She is the calming force in the family. His concentration on business is so complete that he can be absent minded. Once he told her to wait inside a building while he went to get the car. It was raining, and he didn't want her to get wet. But he forgot she was waiting and drove home without her. When he remembered, he hurried back to get her. Gloria has even described him as a superhuman. He was always getting up at the crack of dawn to take care of "a million projects."[2] But when the truck crashed into the Estefans' tour bus, Emilio suddenly found himself helpless.

A nurse who had been caught in the traffic jam came aboard the bus and asked if anyone was

Together, Emilio and Gloria Estefan have built a highly lucrative business empire. Gloria credits their complementary personalities for their success in marriage and business.

hurt. Gloria said she thought her back was broken. She was in terrific pain. The nurse told not to move. But Estefan actually couldn't move much, so powerful and terrifying was the pain in her body. She recalled how her father had spent years as a complete invalid confined to a wheelchair and bed. She thought she didn't want to live if that was to be her fate. "I've always had this gnawing fear. I insisted we install an elevator when we built our home two years ago, even though it is only two stories. Always in the back of my mind I wanted it to be there if I ever needed it. There was always this fear of something happening. . . . I've always attributed that fear to having lived through it with my father," Gloria said.[3]

Paramedics arrived and strapped her onto a board, making sure her head and neck were immobilized. They took her off the bus through the hole left after the front windshield had been smashed to bits. Reporters were already on hand, ready to broadcast and report the accident to the world. Celebrity Gloria Estefan had been severely injured in a crash.

She was taken to a nearby hospital, the Community Medical Center Regional Trauma Center in Scranton, Pennsylvania. There, the trauma team took X rays and a CAT scan. Doctors discovered she had suffered one broken vertebra in her lower back and a partial dislocation of another vertebra near her waist. She didn't know it at the time, but one of her fallopian tubes had been crushed, too. She would need it repaired when she decided to get pregnant again.

The news went out from the hospital. Emilio

wanted all the details out in the open. Right away, too, messages of concern and encouragement came in from as far away as England, where Gloria was a popular figure. George Bush sent a message from the White House. Other celebrated singers and entertainers called the hospital.

When Emilio found out that Gloria had actually broken her back, he fainted. He had a broken rib and a dislocated shoulder, but he didn't even worry about his injuries. Doctors believed Gloria had a good chance for recovery. She had some numbness and weakness and strange sensations in her feet and skin. But she could move a little. Doctors told her she had two choices. She could either spend six months in a body cast and have some physical limitations in the long run, or she could have an operation right away. The operation would probably result in a complete recovery. But she would also run some risks. Infection and paralysis were two of them. Gloria decided on the surgery, because it would give her the chance to get back on her feet fairly quickly.

Estefan's courage, spirit, and drive had been tested before when she had been little more than a child. She later told a reporter of her thoughts at the time: "I don't care about money. I don't care about anything except health. It's the only thing I want. That's why I can't let it [paralysis] happen.

It's not going to happen."[4] She had danced around on stages for years. Now all she wanted was to live a normal life as a wife and mother.

Emilio and Nayib were quickly treated and released from the hospital. Doctors helped Emilio find an orthopedic surgeon who specialized in spinal injuries. The next day, Gloria was transferred by air to New York City's Orthopedic Institute Hospital for Joint Diseases. Aloft in the helicopter with Gloria, Emilio noticed the sunlight shining on them through the windows. He jotted down the phrase, "Coming Out Of The Dark," on a piece of paper and put it away.

At the New York hospital, Gloria was greeted not only by her mother but by Celia Cruz, a famous Cuban-born singer who also had found stardom in the United States. Also on hand was Dr. Michael Neuwirth, the doctor who would perform the operation on Estefan. Neuwirth told the family that he had performed many similar operations. They were complex, but they were routine for him. He said the operation would take about three hours and theorized that Gloria would probably be able to sing and dance around on stage as usual one day. "I think her prognosis is excellent for recovery," he said.[5]

No sooner had Gloria arrived at the hospital than the flowers, cards, and calls began to flood in. Gloria kept a few flowers for herself and sent the rest to other patients and to a Veterans Administration hospital. Her father had been a patient in a VA hospital for years. Her family prayed for her recovery, and Gloria's fan club gathered at a church in Coconut Grove, Florida, and said prayers, too.

Dr. Neuwirth operated on Gloria on March 22, two days after her accident. He fixed two eight-inch-long metal rods on either side of her spinal column to stabilize it. The procedure straightened out her back and relieved the pressure. With a bone graft from her hip, Neuwirth repaired her damaged vertebra.

When Gloria woke from the surgery, she didn't want to look at the long scar down her back at first. She was busy praying that she wouldn't be paralyzed. But on March 23, the good news began to spread. First, Dr. Neuwirth said the operation had been a success. Gloria would recover fully in three to six months. She would be able to leave the hospital in about ten days. After hearing that Gloria's surgery had gone well, Emilio kissed a nurse then wandered aimlessly through the streets of New York for a while to clear his head.

According to a *New York Times* article on March 29, 1990, Gloria had "walked without the aid of crutches or a cane" the day before. "She's doing really well," said Evelyn Torres, a spokeswoman for the hospital. "Her spirits are up, and there's no paralysis at all."[6]

Two weeks later, she was wheeled in a chair to face the reporters who had been besieging the hospital. It seemed as if the whole world wanted to know how she was. Everyone was praying for her recovery. Even people who knew nothing about pop music and had never heard of her until the day of her terrible accident were rooting for her. Upon leaving the hospital, Estefan said to her well-wishers, "I'll see you back on the road." Then she shocked everyone by getting up from the chair and standing on her feet.[7]

> **Even people who knew nothing about pop music . . . were rooting for her.**

Her friend, singer Julio Iglesias, flew her to Miami in his private plane. There, on Emilio's arm, she walked slowly, in pain even with painkillers, down the steps of the plane and stood to make a speech to all the people who had shown up to greet her. She told them, "I want you to know I've felt every one of your prayers from the first moment." She also joked that she hoped the metal in her back didn't set off alarms every time she went through security checks in airports.[8] Keeping her chin up for the 50 reporters and 200 fans

Gloria Estefan smiles as she rises from her wheelchair at an April 1990 press conference following her successful back surgery. It would be many months of painful rehabilitation before Estefan could perform again.

who showed up to welcome her, she said she was glad she had gotten a day with sunshine for her homecoming.

A reporter noticed that she winced with pain when she sat back down in her wheelchair. The doctor had put more than 400 stitches in her back. Muscles had been cut during the operation. Every 45 minutes at night, she and Emilio had to get up and walk around their luxurious home on Star Island in Miami to keep her muscles from stiffening up. "She used to walk and cry at the same time," Emilio told a writer for *McCall's* magazine. "It was very tough."[9]

CHAPTER TWO

A NEW LIFE IN MIAMI

The first challenge in Gloria's life began not long after her second birthday. In late 1959, young Gloria Maria Fajardo was set in her seat on a Pan American Airways plane leaving her birthplace of Havana, Cuba, for Miami, Florida. With her were her mother, also named Gloria, and father, José Manuel Fajardo. A few years earlier, the trip would have been a treat, but this was a necessity. Cuba's dictatorial government had been overthrown by rebels, led by Fidel Castro.

José Fajardo, a good-looking, well-built man, had been a member of the security forces protecting Cuba's dictator, Fulgencio Batista. This position qualified Fajardo as a member of the middle class, the fate of which was unknown under the new regime. Castro was a Communist who intended to nationalize all property and assets in

Cuba. This meant that only the government could own anything.

José Fajardo and his wife believed it would be dangerous for them to remain in Cuba. They decided to seek political refuge in Miami, along with hundreds of thousands of other Cubans, and hoped they could one day return to Cuba and resume their happy lives there. So they bought round-trip tickets. As it turned out, that trip was one-way.

Gloria, who was born on September 1, 1957, was too young to have gotten much of an impression of her home in Havana. Only 90 miles away, Miami didn't make much of an impression either. The sunlight was bright. The Florida landscape was filled with palm trees. And the warm breezes blew in Miami exactly the way they did in Havana.

But her parents knew the difference immediately. First of all, they were forced to live in conditions they had never known before: They were suddenly poor. With other refugees from Cuba, they turned one neighborhood of Miami into a community that was quickly nicknamed Little Havana. The area, located in northwest Miami, had simple, one- and two-story buildings filled with small four-room apartments. The buildings were in a neglected condition and were laid out in a regular, geometric pattern, with no attempt to

*Members of Fidel Castro's revolutionary army prepare
for their takeover of the Cuban government, forcing
thousands of nonsympathetic Cubans, including
Gloria Estefan's parents, to flee the island.*

make them pretty. Over the years, the inhabitants
spruced up their new home. But little more than
some grass and a few tropical plants suggested
the lushness of the Miami and Miami Beach
neighborhoods where the well-to-do lived and the

tourists frolicked in the swimming pools and the ocean.

Not long after the family arrived in Miami, José Fajardo left his wife and child behind to join the U.S. government's military invasion of Cuba. President John F. Kennedy planned to send a fighting force of Cuban refugees back to their homeland to stir up an insurrection against Castro and his left-wing government. José Fajardo went with the other troops to Guatemala in Central America to train for the battle. From the outset, the plan had little chance of success.

Nevertheless, the invasion began April 1961. U.S. forces launched air strikes to help the brigade of Cuban exiles. But the air strikes suddenly stopped, dooming the mission to failure. José Fajardo was nearly killed in a tank, but a comrade saved him. He was then captured, along with many others, by the Cuban army.

For a year and a half, José Fajardo suffered in a Cuban jail. Gloria's mother wrote to her husband, but the letters came back. The Cuban government refused to acknowledge it was holding prisoners. Gloria's mother didn't want to tell her daughter that José was in jail. That was too harsh. So she said José was working on a farm. Gloria probably found out the truth anyway, because everyone in Little Havana was talking about the event.

Gloria Estefan poses here with her mother, Gloria Fajardo. With her soldier husband often gone, Fajardo raised Gloria and sister Rebecca on her own for much of their early childhood.

Gloria later told Leonard Pitts Jr., a music critic with the *Miami Herald,* that she grew up in a community of women—the wives and female relatives of the men imprisoned in Cuba. "We were here in an apartment behind the Orange Bowl, all the women with their kids. No husbands. One car that cost $50. They'd pile us all in the car and go do the shopping." Gloria knew that sometimes her mother was hungry, but she made sure that Gloria got good, regular meals.

In late 1962, José Fajardo finally came home after Castro agreed to trade the prisoners for millions of dollars worth of supplies that he needed from the United States. The men came home just in time for Christmas, thus ending the military adventure and catastrophe now known as the Bay of Pigs. But José Fajardo and his friends still longed for a day when they could try again. They hoped that Castro would somehow be forced out of power, and they could return to their homeland. Many became totally devoted to convincing the U.S. government to help make their dream come true.

Gloria tried to adjust to her new country. She listened to Spanish songs sung by her family and neighbors or played at community gatherings. The music was beautiful. But it saddened her, because she saw how emotional people became when they listened to it. She preferred to listen to American pop music. As Estefan has noted in interviews, she particularly admired Johnny Mathis, Barbra Streisand, Diana Ross, and Karen Carpenter. Music lifted her spirits. She even loved the song "Ferry Cross the Mersey" by the British pop group Gerry and the Pacemakers, though she had no idea what the Mersey was. She loved the melodies and harmonies and the styles with which the singers communicated their messages. And she was particularly attracted to the easy-listening, mellow voice of Karen Carpenter.

She loved the melodies and harmonies and the styles with which the singers communicated their messages.

While her father was imprisoned, Gloria and her mother lived primarily on money provided by the U.S. government—probably money that had been slated to be José Fajardo's salary. When Fajardo came back, he joined the U.S. Army. The family lived moved to Fort Jackson, South Carolina, and then to San Antonio, Texas. In 1964, the Fajardos welcomed another child, Rebecca. The family called her Becky; and Gloria made up the nickname Beckski.

In 1966, José volunteered for a two-year tour of duty in Vietnam, hoping that his service would help convince the U.S. government to do more to help the Cubans return to their homeland. Gloria

Gloria Estefan and sister Rebecca.

was separated from her father again, but she sent him audio tapes filled with family news and songs.

"I sent him a lot of songs. He would love it because he played it for the guys who were with him on the base. They would all cry," Estefan said much later.[1] He once sent her back a tape saying, "One day you're going to be a great star."[2]

Apparently noticing how much her eldest daughter loved music, Gloria's mother gave her a guitar when she turned nine. The family had a tradition of loving music. Gloria's family, which may have come originally from the Asturias region of Spain,[3] included a classical violinist and a salsa pianist who played Cuban music on her father's side, and "two uncles who sang and wrote their own songs," Gloria said.[4]

Gloria's mother "won an international song and dance contest, and was to be Shirley Temple's double and dub her movies, both spoken words and songs in Spanish," Gloria told an interviewer. "Her father, however, was a very strict Spaniard, who didn't like the idea of his daughter going to Hollywood. So he told her she couldn't do it and nipped her career in the bud."

Gloria nurtured her love affair with music by listening to pop music on the radio and records of traditional Cuban music in the family's collection.[5] She began to teach herself the guitar and studied songbooks in the public library. She had such a strong interest in music that her parents urged her to take classical guitar lessons. So she had a bit of formal training.

When José Fajardo returned from Vietnam in 1968, it seemed that the family's fortunes would brighten. But soon after his homecoming, he began to have trouble with his balance. "He'd fall for no reason. Or he'd stop for a red light, but the light would be green. My mother made him go to the hospital for tests. When he came out, he was already walking with a cane," Gloria said.[6]

He was diagnosed with multiple sclerosis, a degenerative neuromuscular disease. He had been a strapping, athletic man but soon became dependent on his family to help him with all his daily chores. He couldn't work; he couldn't even wash and dress himself properly. Gloria later came to believe that his illness had actually been caused by exposure to poisonous chemicals in Vietnam. The job of helping him fell to Gloria, as she began her teen years. Her sister Becky also looked to Gloria for special care and affect. Their mother, who had been a teacher in Cuba, went back to school and became certified to teach in Miami's public schools. The nightmare of seeing her father fading away made Gloria feel helpless and lonely. She bolstered her morale by singing songs.

"It was my release from everything, my escape. I'd lock myself in my room with my guitar.

I wouldn't cry. I was afraid if I let go just a little bit, it would all go. I would sing for hours by myself," Gloria later told an interviewer. "Music was the only way I had to just let go, so I sang—for fun and for emotional catharsis."[7]

> **"Music was the only way I had to just let go, so I sang—for fun and for emotional catharsis."**

Whether it was her father's illness, or her tendency to take after the quiet man, or her feelings about being a new immigrant in a strange land, she became shy and reserved. She thought she had these personality traits because she was her father's daughter. She even began to worry that she would become physically disabled herself one day. Seeing the tragedy so close up filled her with dread and wisdom about what a burden a person could become. She didn't begrudge her father the care she gave him. She loved him and wanted to help. So did her mother and sister Rebecca. But José Fajardo didn't improve with the loving care. The worse he got, the more Gloria turned to music as a comfort.

She was also surrounded by the sadness of the older people who dreamed of returning to Cuba. That was her father's great dream, too. She knew it would never come true. By the time she was sixteen, in 1973, her father's condition worsened so much that the family was forced to put him in the Veterans' Administration Hospital. There, he could get the professional nursing care that he now required.

Music, especially American pop music, gave Estefan the inspiration to overcome the sadness in her life by becoming a part of the American dream. As much as she sympathized with the older generation, she had never really known the old country. At the same time, she knew that some native-born Americans often complained about the flood of new immigrants. She could at least dream about becoming rich, successful, and beloved in her adopted country.[8]

CHAPTER THREE

MEETING EMILIO

Gloria was so shy as a student at Lourdes Academy, a Catholic girls high school, that the nuns thought she would become a nun herself. She had no boyfriends. But she really had no notion of becoming a nun. Instead she applied and was accepted to the University of Miami, where she began studying communications and psychology on a partial scholarship. And she continued to sing, often in harmony with her cousin, Mercedes—"Merci," as she was called. When the girls met a couple of other like-minded people, they decided to try to put together a group and hire themselves out on weekends. Many talented amateur Cuban musicians earned a little extra money this way. Estefan and her friends entertained at dances and parties, but soon found that they needed a strong guiding hand.

That hand belonged to a young man named

Emilio Estefan Jr., who was four years older than Gloria and whose family also had relocated to Miami. His early life had been filled with troubles, too, but he never gave into them. He was a friendly, smiling fellow who kept his courage up. The very private Estefan has not made the details of his life known, but he either was born in Lebanon in the Middle East and migrated as a boy with his parents to Cuba, or else his parents were born in Lebanon and migrated to Cuba before his birth. In any case, the Estefan family lived in Santiago de Cuba, a sleepy town with a great African heritage located at the other end of the island from Havana. When Castro came to power, the Estefan family didn't leave the country right away. Emilio's father had a job in a clothing factory, so the revolution didn't upset the Estefan family's life the way it did the fortunes of middle-class and wealthy Cubans.

But when it became plain that Castro was going to draft the eldest Estefan son into the army, Emilio's father decided to take him to Europe in about 1973. They settled in Spain and tried to make their way, but times were very tough. Some days they had nothing to eat unless they went to places that gave away free meals to the impoverished.

Emilio had taught himself to play the accordion in Santiago de Cuba. And that ability helped save his life in Spain. He played music in restaurants to earn enough money to feed himself and his father. After a time, the elder Estefan made plans for Emilio to emigrate to the United States to stay in Miami with an aunt. By the mid-1970s, Emilio began his life in America by sleeping on the floor with his numerous cousins in his aunt's apartment.

He didn't waste any time in planning for a better life for himself. Every day, at 7 A.M., he began work in the mail room at the Bacardi Imports company in Miami. At night, he went to high school. He also took out a loan to buy a very good accordion, and he played it in an Italian restaurant every night for tips. All these activities filled his days. By 1975, he and two friends had formed a group called the Miami Latin Boys; they played on weekends for parties, dances, weddings—anything that needed traditional Cuban music.

Then a coworker at Bacardi asked Emilio to help a new group get started. In it was the coworker's son, as was Gloria Fajardo and her cousin Merci. Gloria always remembers her first meeting with Emilio very clearly. When he came to coach the new group, he was carrying his accordion and wearing a pair of very short shorts. "I thought he was cute," Gloria said years later.[1]

They met again about three months later

when Emilio's band was hired to play for a wedding reception in Hialeah. Gloria and her mother were guests there. According to one version of the story, Emilio spotted Gloria right away. Later he would say that he had always thought she had beautiful eyes and a fine complexion. He asked her to sing with his group at the wedding. Gloria refused, but he coaxed her. She sang some songs in Spanish, including the popular love song, "Sabor a Mí."

Emilio got the bright idea to ask Gloria to join his band. None of the weekend salsa bands—bands playing Spanish-language pop with roots in Cuban music—had female singers. The novelty of having a female singer appealed to Emilio—but not to Gloria. She wanted to focus on her studies at the University of Miami. But Emilio wouldn't take no for an answer. He and his mother, by then living in Miami, had a meeting with Gloria's family. And they decided that Gloria could sing with the band on the weekends, as long as her cousin Merci also sang. In the protective Cuban family tradition, Gloria had to have a chaperone.

The band forced the quiet teenagers, Gloria and Merci, to attend many social gatherings, for

Emilio got the bright idea to ask Gloria to join his band.

which live music was an indispensable part. Audiences enjoyed the singing cousins. Emilio, who was not a great musician and had never learned to read music, let the girls take an increasingly prominent role, while he moved into the background. The little bit of money the group earned helped Gloria. She also took a job as a Spanish language interpreter for the U.S. Customs Service.[2] She was still concentrating on her practical goal of getting a degree in psychology from the University of Miami.

During the year when Emilio and Gloria began working together, they realized they were in love. But they didn't even kiss. For a while, Emilio had a girlfriend who was older than he was. And Gloria was an innocent schoolgirl. On the night of the Bicentennial celebration—the 200th anniversary of the United States in 1976—the Miami Latin Boys were scheduled to perform on a ship, the *Miss Florida*. Emilio had never told Gloria that he was in love with her. But as he was driving her to the ship, he said, "You know, if we got married, I'd bet we'd get along very well."[3] She was very surprised and didn't answer him.

Later that night, when they watched the fireworks together, Emilio followed up his shocking proposal with the claim that it was his birthday. He said, "I think you should give me a birthday kiss," Gloria recalled.[4] They bargained about it.

A combination of Latin rhythms and catchy pop tunes brought the Miami Sound Machine to worldwide attention in the 1980s.

He finally got her to agree to kiss him on the cheek. When she moved toward him, he turned and kissed her on the lips.

It was not a whirlwind romance. Taking their time, the couple arranged their wedding for

September 2, 1978. In the interim, they tended to business. A record producer suggested the group change its name to include the women, and the Miami Latin Boys became the Miami Sound Machine. The group made its first self-produced recording—with a few thousand dollars that Emilio scraped together—entirely in Spanish in 1977. During the next two years, they made two more Spanish language recordings.

Two years after their marriage, Emilio and Gloria further solidified their personal relationship when Gloria gave birth to their first child, Nayib. The group became even more of a family affair when cousin Merci married the keyboardist, Raul Murciano.

Emilio kept his job at Bacardi all the while because the group didn't earn enough money to pay the bills. But the recordings, with their hybrid sound combining Latin, Cuban, and American pop music, were making the group popular in Miami. Everyone who knew Emilio observed what a great entrepreneur he was. He rose to an important job in the marketing department of Bacardi. And he had a knack for promoting projects of all kinds.

The Miami Sound Machine was just one of many groups in Miami. But Emilio, the group's manager, made three unusual and important moves. First he incorporated the group and held controlling interest. The remaining shares belonged to the other members of the group. Second, Emilio signed a contract for the group with CBS Discos International, the Hispanic division of CBS Records based in Miami. The Miami Sound Machine would record pop songs in the Spanish language for the label for sale in Latin America. So the group began to build its reputation in Latin America.

By the mid-1980s, the Miami Sound Machine became so hot that some of its recordings topped the charts in several Central and South American countries. And as usual, Emilio kept the band working all the time. In that way, the group began to make real headway, outdoing all the other Miami-based bands.

Also by that time, Emilio quit his job at Bacardi so he could devote all his time to managing the group. That's how much he believed in its possibilities. And they were finally earning enough money to inspire him. Unfortunately, success spoiled the group's relationships, with some of the band members on one side, and Emilio and Gloria on the other side. The band members didn't think Emilio was paying them enough money. Raul Murciano quit the band, and his wife Merci followed soon after.

One groupmember who stayed, drummer Enrique "Kiki" García, had the talent to write the song that would help the Miami Sound Machine break into the mainstream of the music world. The tune, called "Dr. Beat," was a simple but very rhythmic number with lyrics about people who couldn't stop their feet from dancing. Emilio thought it would be just the right song to attract attention in the crossover market—the market for all Americans, not just Hispanics. Executives at CBS didn't think the song was very good. Nevertheless, "Dr. Beat" became a big hit. Its success prompted the company to put out the first English language album for the Miami Sound Machine, *Eyes of Innocence.*

Then Emilio heard another drummer, José Galdo, who was playing with a group called The Jerks. Emilio invited him to bring his musicians into the Miami Sound Machine. Galdo's musicians added the needed quality to the Miami Sound Machine's recordings. And drummer Kiki García wrote another crossover hit called "Conga" based on a traditional Cuban dance rhythm. This tune, which appeared on the group's second English-language album, *Primitive Love*, went gold (meaning it sold a half million copies) and put the Miami Sound Machine prominently on the map. And the song "Conga" pulled off a crossover miracle. It rose to the top of four chart categories—Latin, R&B, Dance, and Pop.

Whenever the group played, "Conga" was always top on the audiences' request list. During a show in Burlington, Vermont, 11,000 people formed a conga line as the band performed the hit. Then, in an annual festival on Calle Ocho—Eighth Street—in Little Havana in Miami, nearly 120,000 people formed an even longer conga line. The event made the Guinness Book of World Records. And Gloria Estefan and the Miami Sound Machine led the line.

The group's repertoire continued to be a clever blending of Cuban traditions and American pop, of ballads and highly charged rhythm songs. Cuban music is exceptionally complex, and the Miami Sound Machine could not present all its rich and diverse rhythms, some of them rooted in the ceremonies of the Afro-Cuban religion Santería. But there was enough of a taste of Cuba's powerful, emotionally driving, and exciting musical legacy to give the Miami Sound Machine its distinctive appeal.

As the group's fortunes were rising, Emilio made another change. For its next album, *Let It Loose,* Gloria Estefan's name was added to the group's official name. The Miami Sound Machine was now Gloria Estefan (in big letters) and the Miami Sound Machine. Critics accepted the change in emphasis, because Gloria singing style was distinct enough to give her prominence. The ballad, "Can't Stay Away From You," which Estefan wrote, was particularly appealing to critics.

This time, the album sold several million copies worldwide.[5]

Generally, although the members all came from Cuban refugee families, the Miami Sound Machine steered away from politics and political songs. Nevertheless, when the group was invited to play at the Pan American Games in Indianapolis in August 1987, the competitors from Cuba

The band, now Gloria Estefan and the Miami Sound Machine, performs at the 1987 Pan American Games in Indianapolis, despite protests from the Cuban delegation.

protested. The mere presence of a music group consisting of Cuban refugees had political implications for Castro. The Cubans even threatened to boycott the games if the group sang. The Cubans didn't want any refugee groups involved in the celebration. That's how high feelings ran between the exiles and the pro-Castro Cubans.

In the end, the Miami Sound Machine sang at the finale for the games. The Cubans, who did attend, sat still in their seats while crowds danced and cheered wildly for the group. Estefan, mindful of the sacrifices her father had made for Cuba, announced to reporters that the Miami Sound Machine symbolized the success of Cubans in a free country.

Emilio's efforts on behalf of Gloria and himself paid off royally. Through his negotiations, he and Gloria earned most of the profits of the band, and as the group prospered, the Estefans became rich. The band had its first Grammy nomination for its album in 1984. But because most of the band's money went to the Estefans, and Gloria now had top billing, the men in the band felt they weren't sharing enough in the success. They began to quit. First José "Joe" Galdo and the Jerks left. Then Kiki García quit the band after a tour to promote the album *Let It Loose*.

Despite such upsets, most people liked the Estefans. Cuban-born jazz saxophonist Paquito

D'Rivera, who worked with them on several occasions, considered Emilio Estefan a genius for building such a successful group and for turning Gloria Estefan into its diva. And he considered Gloria a fine role model as a wife and mother and community-minded person—"a nice person," he said. Even Joe Galdo had loved working with Gloria. She was never temperamental and always willing to work hard.

People liked Emilio, too. Record company people realized that he had the vision, energy, and ambition needed to push the band forward. He met with a lot of resistance from North American recording company directors at first. But he had made all the deals and arrangements for the band. He could take credit for the success of choosing the musicians and composers. If he also had to stand up to criticism for taking a great deal of the profits for himself and his family, well, the record company people knew all was fair in love and war—and in the music business. As a good businessman, Emilio had done the right things.

By the late 1980s, Gloria Estefan was truly approaching the top of her profession. Always on the move, she performed at the World Series in St. Louis in 1987. In July

By the late 1980s, Gloria Estefan was truly approaching the top of her profession.

1988, she took part in the First New York International Festival of the Arts in Central Park. No less a star than famed operatic tenor Placido Domingo was host. She sang a duet with him and then delivered her own song, "Anything For You," a big hit from the album *Let It Loose*. (Four songs from that album made the top ten.) And "she did it neatly," wrote John Rockwell, in a review for the *New York Times*.[6]

Critic Stephen Holden wrote that he enjoyed the band's "perky middle of the road music that reflects the assimilation of the Cuban emigré population into the city from which (the Miami Sound Machine) takes its name." By that time, *Let It Loose* had sold nearly two million copies. Holden said that Gloria's voice on "Anything For You" reminded him of the sound of pop star Karen Carpenter. "The evening's liveliest moment was an exuberant performance of 'Conga,' the group's first and most rhythmically animated American hit. Performed by a nine-member ensemble that included three horn players and two percussionists, it transplanted the exuberant ambiance of a Havana nightclub directly to Manhattan."[7]

Gloria traveled as far as the demilitarized zone between South and North Korea on her "Let It Loose" tour to entertain the troops with her hits. Her final concert in that tour played to a "standing room only" crowd at the Miami Arena, and it was broadcast on cable television's Show-time and won three Cable Ace awards.[8]

Also in 1988, the Estefan's built a multimillion-dollar home, complete with an elevator, on Miami Beach's exclusive Star Island. The addition of household staff freed the Estefans to raise their son, work on their careers, and entertain friends. Their lifestyle was a far cry from the days when Emilio had slept on the floor in his aunt's house, and Gloria and her family had lived in cramped quarters in the shadow of the Orange Bowl.

The Estefans' multimillion-dollar home is located on Star Island, an exclusive neighborhood near Miami.

CHAPTER FOUR

COMING OUT OF THE DARK

In 1990, Gloria Estefan was on top of the world and the pop music charts. But the accident that broke her back changed all that. She and Emilio had worked so hard to get where they were, and now they would have to start all over again, in another way. "When you go from having everything anybody could possibly want to being overjoyed at putting on your underwear, it drives a lot of things home," Estefan said about her six-month struggle to regain the ability to do even the simplest tasks.[1] Her return to walking was a major victory. Then she moved up to being able to lean over the sink and wash her face herself. Another day she could put on high-heeled shoes and stand in them. Still another day she could put her weight on her left foot again.

Estefan had physical therapy three days a week. A trainer helped her work out in the swimming pool to strengthen her arms and legs. Emilio drove her, wearing her back brace, to a massage therapist. She had wanted to take time off to try to relax and become pregnant again, but that plan went on hold. All her energies went toward her recovery. She focused on her goal of going on the road again. Little by little, she won the battle.

It was discovered that the trailer of the truck that hit them had defective brakes, so Emilio Estefan filed lawsuits against everyone connected with the accident—the truck driver, the company he worked for, the company for which he was carrying cargo, and others. There was a court battle in Scranton, Pennsylvania, at which doctors and others testified, and the Estefan's emerged victorious. The settlement came to nearly $9 million dollars. Of that, the Estefan's received $8.3 million. Nayib got $150,000; Gloria's assistant, who also was injured, received $100,000, and Nayib's tutor got $20,000. The figures were based to some extent on the estimated amount of money Gloria lost by not performing. She may have lost $500,000 to $2 million in box office receipts for each concert, depending upon the city where she would have been singing.[2] To show her gratitude, Gloria presented a check for $5,000 to the Ronald McDonald House in Scranton, where her family had stayed while she was in the hospital there.

By the time of the settlement, it was 1993.

Estefan had long since fought her way back into the light. But right after her accident, Emilio hadn't been able to interest her in singing or writing music again. She just didn't feel like it. But he had a surprise for her. During their helicopter ride to New York Hospital, he had jotted down the words "coming out of the dark," when sunlight flooded the plane. Now, on Star Island, he pulled out the paper and read the words to her. As if by magic, they inspired her.

Soon, she was writing a song. Then she began working with Miami Sound Machine musicians and backup singers for a new album. She planned her first public appearance for the American Music Awards, broadcast on TV in January, 1991—less than a year after the accident. She wasn't nominated for an award that year. But when she appeared to present an award to someone else, the studio audience gave her a standing ovation.

Soon, she was writing a song.

In 1991, her new album, *Into the Light,* featuring her song "Coming Out of the Dark," was released. That was followed by the "Into The Light" tour. Estefan chose Lakeland, Florida, for a dress-rehearsal site for her opening show and performed before a group of 100 disabled adults in February. They applauded so much for her that she said, "Oh, my God, you guys sound like ten thousand people. We definitely picked the right people."[3] On March 1, 1991, she officially opened the tour at the Miami Arena and played to more than 12,000 fans. Gloria wore a blue-sequined dress and a glittering mask, with her long brown hair curling and buoyant around her smiling face.

Estefan began a world tour in 1991 after fully recovering from her accident. Her concerts were sellouts everywhere she played.

When she took off the mask, the audience shouted and stood up. Gloria's first song was "Get On Your Feet." Then she sang "Coming Out Of The Dark" and a Cuban folk song, "Oye Mi Canto." She brought her son, Nayib, onstage when she performed "Nayib's Song," her tribute to him. And she dedicated her song, "Anything for You," to Dr. Michael Neuwirth, the surgeon who fixed her back. He was backstage for the show, were he told a reporter, "Now she has to perform, not me."[4] She also dedicated songs to the crowd, and her voice was clear and strong. She could dance again, too. Doctors had told her she had very few limitations; she couldn't sky dive or play football—but she had never in her wildest dreams ever wanted to do these things anyway. "I love you, Miami," she told the crowd.

After Miami, the tour moved to Europe. In London, all of Gloria's shows were sold out, and the crowds adored her in other European cities, too. By June, 1991, the courageous singer was back in the White House, invited once again by her admirer, President George Bush, to perform at a state dinner honoring Brazilian president Fernando Collor de Mello.

But Gloria's battles didn't end with her physical recovery or the settlement of her lawsuit. In 1989, bandleader Eddie Palmieri accused her of plagiarizing his song "Páginas de Mujer," which he claimed she had released as "Oye Mi Canto" on her 1989 album *Cuts Both Ways*. Palmieri, himself a Grammy winner, had written and recorded a song ten years earlier that he claimed Gloria had copied. Palmieri sued her for about $10 million dollars, based on the worldwide sales of Gloria's song. In the suit, Palmieri claimed that Gloria had heard his recording and used it to compose her own song.

It's possible Gloria actually had heard his recording, but she said she never did. A couple of musicians in Miami and even Emilio Estefan's brother, José, said it was possible Gloria had heard the song. But nobody could offer any proof. Gloria said she listened only to the pop music radio station in Miami, not the station that played Cuban music and Palmieri's songs. Both her song and Palmieri's contained elements of an older Cuban song, a folk song, and that meant it was in the public domain and legally available for anyone to sing and record.

Palmieri did have some interesting facts on his side. He had sold 2,000 copies of his record in the Miami area and 40,000 nationwide. And his status in the Latin music community made it possible, even perhaps likely, that Estefan had heard his song before she wrote her own. Both Estefans knew Palmieri and had told him they counted among his fans. The case dragged out for years, and Palmieri eventually dropped his charges. Palmieri's record sales and popularity constituted his strongest evidence. But it was rather more circumstantial than hard proof. No one had ever seen Gloria reading or listening to his music.

There was one thing the suit did prove: José Estefan, who testified at pretrial hearings, revealed that he had very hard, angry feelings against his brother, Emilio. In 1979, Emilio and Gloria Estefan had somehow gotten permission to travel to Cuba to help José get out. They were unsuccessful, but they did come back with reports of the desperate living conditions suffered by most Cubans. Emilio Estefan continued his efforts to bring his brother to the United States, however, and in the early 1980s he was successful.

When José Estefan arrived in Miami, Emilio hired him and gave him major responsibilities in Estefan Enterprises, the family business. But according to José, he was eventually fired, and he claimed that Emilio was stingy and unfair to him and to other employees. José said it was possible that Gloria had heard Palmieri's song, but he had no real proof. Although the publicity surrounding the trial consisted of little more than rumors about the plagiarism charges, the Estefans were greatly disturbed. They had been developing a reputation for giving money and help to the needy.[5]

Even though the case never went to a trial,

many tough questions were raised. Did Gloria plagiarize Palmieri's creation? Was Emilio trustworthy? Did the allegations have some basis in fact?—or were they the result of jealousy? It would not have been the first time that very successful celebrities found themselves besieged by people motivated by jealousy who made false accusations in the hopes of getting money. And a great deal of money was at stake. These questions were never answered and remain so.

By the 1990s, the Estefans owned several hotels in the Miami area and a restaurant at Disney World in Orlando. The Estefan property on Star Island was estimated to be worth about $24 million. And the net worth of the empire Emilio built around Gloria was estimated at figures ranging from $50 million upward to $170 million.[6] Emilio's businesses include real estate holdings, such as the Cardozo hotel in Miami's trendy South Beach, a café, and a Cuban restaurant as well as Estefan Enterprises Inc., an entertainment and promotion company, and the Crescent Moon Studio, a Miami recording studio.

For sure, neither José Estefan nor Eddie Palmieri nor any of the Miami Sound Machine musicians had ever come close to matching the success of Gloria and Emilio Estefan. The couple's story was a miracle, a rags-to-riches tale representing the legendary American dream. Legions of fans adored Gloria. They praised her character and down-to-earth personality. Her Cuban fans in Miami particularly were thrilled about her success. She had come from their ranks. She was one of them, and with great pride, they claimed her and called her "Nuestra Glorita" (Our Little Gloria).

In discussing her relationship with her husband, Estefan noted, "We have always worked together, and that has cemented our relationship. This is not just a career, it's a lifestyle, and being together has been instrumental in our success. Also, it helps that we have the same values and want the same things out of life. We also have similar interests outside of our work."[7] Usually Gloria defers to his judgment where business matters are concerned. But if she doesn't like one of his ideas involving her, whether related to business or music, she tells

> **Sometimes, Estefan confided, when he [Emilio] comes home, he calls out to Gloria, "Lucy, I'm home."**

him. Sometimes she has the last word. And Estefan has said she finds it romantic to work so closely with her husband.

A profile about Emilio Estefan in the *Miami Herald* revealed his sense of humor, which has also helped their relationship. They named two of their five Dalmations Ricky and Lucy in honor of

Cuban entertainer Desi Arnaz and his wife, American comedian and actress, Lucille Ball, of "I Love Lucy" fame. Sometimes, Estefan confided, when he comes home, he calls out to Gloria, "Lucy, I'm home."

Despite the pressures of their work, the Estefans dine together every night when not on tour and often take hour-long walks afterward. Emilio said, "I'd never do anything without asking her, and she never does anything without asking me. It's not like who's the boss. You have to share your life. . . . I think the basis is love. When you are in love, everything is easy."[8]

CHAPTER FIVE

ILLUSTRIOUS DAYS

"Into the Light" continued selling very well into 1992, but it would not be nominated for a Grammy. That honor still eluded Gloria. Her past Grammy nominations had been for Best Pop Performance for a duo or a group with a vocal, for the song "Anything for You," in Spanish and English, with the Miami Sound Machine in 1988; and for Best Pop Vocal Performance, Female, for the song "Don't Wanna Lose You," in 1989. But Gloria continued her personal appearances, including spectacular halftime show for the 1992 Super Bowl between the Washington Redskins and the Buffalo Bills football teams at the Metrodome in Minneapolis, Minnesota.

Later that year, Gloria's talents were called upon for a different and unexpected task—helping the Florida victims of Hurricane Andrew, which struck in late August. When weather reports made it clear that the very powerful storm was going to hit the Miami area, the Estefans, Gloria's mother, and some friends—even the Estefan household pets—retreated from Star Island and took refuge in the Estefans' studio, Crescent Moon, in the city of Miami. Gloria later told the *Miami Herald,* "At one point at about three in the morning, the whole building got sucked to one side. I was lying on the couch, and my back got plastered to the couch. I thought, here we go."[1]

The strong winds tore the radar apparatus off the roof of the National Hurricane Center building and destroyed countless homes and even the nearby Homestead Air Force Base's control tower and airplane hangars. Water, electricity, mail—all these services were put out of commission for a long time. The damage was estimated at more than $16 billion dollars.

Gloria sent a check to the United Way's relief fund for people left homeless by the storm. Then the U.S. Army asked the Estefans if they would visit the devastated South Dade County area on Labor Day to entertain and boost morale among the storm's victims, who were living in tents. Gloria sang and signed autographs for the people. But she decided that was not enough. So she and Emilio joined with other famous entertainers to

Estefan offers assistance to rescue workers in the aftermath of Hurricane Andrew, which caused $16 billion dollars worth of damage in southern Florida.

stage a hurricane-relief concert at the Joe Robbie Stadium in Miami. Some 50,000 people showed up. The concert raised $2 million dollars. Gloria sang her own song, "There Will Always Be Tomorrow," in honor of the event. She also released a video of the song that included an address to which people could mail donations to the hurricane-relief fund.

Such activities brought public attention to Estefan's devotion to humanitarian causes. She won a Humanitarian of the Year award from B'nai B'rith, a leading antidiscrimination organization, in 1992. Also that year, she and Emilio received the Alexis de Toqueville Award from the United Way of Dade County for their volunteer work and commitment to improving the quality of life in their community. They had helped people with their work after Hurricane Andrew, and they had

Estefan performs with comedian/actor Whoopi Goldberg at a 1992 concert to raise money for disaster relief for victims of Hurricane Andrew.

also donated money from concerts to the United Negro College Fund and to the Community Alliance against AIDS.

In September 1992, in recognition of her service to the people of South Florida and her other community projects, such as her antidrug work, President George Bush chose her as an honorary delegate from the United States to the United Nations. In October, the Senate confirmed Bush's nomination of Estefan, and she joined the ranks of other entertainers, such as singer Pearl Bailey.

Estefan took the job seriously, showing up on time for her assignments and delivering speeches that the United States Mission prepared for her. One speech dealt with relief for refugees from all sorts of disasters, such as war and famine, around the globe. Estefan first spoke in favor of United States support for increased funding for refugees under the program called the United Nations High Commission on Refugees. She then delivered a speech about the importance of freedom of the press and expression. In November 1992, she gave a speech in Spanish in support of the Voice of America, a government run radio station that sends pro-democracy broadcasts to foreign countries perceived to be communist in political organization, and in defense of freedom of the press and of access to information. By implication, she included the border of the 90 miles of water

*In September 1992, then-President George Bush
named Gloria Estefan an honorary delegate
to the United Nations.*

separating the United States from Cuba. Estefan stated that the U.S. government did nothing to block other governments or international voices from finding audiences in the United States. In effect all governments should follow the example of the United States, she said.

Though she didn't mention Cuba or Fidel Castro directly, the Cuban ambassador to the United Nations decided to defend his country. Exercising the right of reply provided by the United Nations, he said his government objected to the U.S. broadcasts to Cuba because Cuba and the United States had no formal agreement about the exchange of information. Estefan's message on behalf of the United States had hit home.

By this time, Estefan considered herself a part of the fabric of American society. "Even though it's a homeland," she said about Cuba, "and I would love for (the people living there) to be free, it would be tough for me, for our generation to go back and really make a name for ourselves or even move back there," she told writer Carol Pugh of the Associated Press.[2]

Normally, Estefan did not involve herself in politics, nor did she put political messages into her songs. But in 1993, she took a turn away from her usual pop repertoire and recorded an album in Spanish called *Mi Tierra*. It was a major project that took most of a year and cost a great deal of money. She sang new songs, but they were presented in a way that suggested the sound of music in old Cuba—the Cuba of the 1930s, 1940s, and even the 1950s before the revolution. Estefan told pop music critic Leonard Pitts Jr. about her reasons for doing the album: "I don't know if it's my age that I'm getting to now, but I have a real deep love of all things Cuban. . . . I think very much along the lines of the Anglo mentality in our work ethic and the way that we do things in our organization. We want to try to be the best that you can be and compete on a world scope. But in my heart and in my music and in my way of life and the way I love and the way I argue and everything, I'm very Cuban. My heart is that."[3]

> **. . . the music of Mi Tierra was Gloria's sentimental voyage into the Cuban past.**

She tapped into such Cuban traditions as the music of the 1930s, with its medium tempos and stringed instruments, and the faster songs that developed in the 1940s. Underlying all the songs were some of the rhythms that had been invented in Cuba through the influence of the people of African descent who had been brought there as slaves. Primarily they had been members of the Yoruba tribe of West Africa and had been brought to Cuba to work in the sugarcane fields.

The uniqueness of Cuban music is in its rhythms. And the percussion instruments, such as the familiar congas, bongos and timbales, differ from those in other countries as well. Cuban music has more force, rhythms, and complexity than the music of other Latin countries. The rhythms called *conga* and *son montuno* form the fast and slow part, respectively, of the evolution of a piece of dance music. Son montuno is called *salsa* in the United States. In any case, son montuno, or salsa, uses the *clave* (pronounced clahvay) as the basis of the rhythm, and so do almost all other types of Cuban music's sixty-one rhythms, including the popular *rumba*. The 3-2 clave is used for son montuno, and the 2-3 clave is used for *guaguancó* and rumba. Each style of music has its own basic rhythm, but the clave can be played with all but one of them.

Pat your hand on the table three times, then two times more. Now pat your hand twice, then three times. Those rhythms are the clave, and they have influenced most of the music of Spanish-speaking America. The clave is a profound, intense rhythmic feeling. And probably the main inspiration for Cuban music comes from the church—especially the Afro-Cuban religions, such as Santería, with its roots in the traditions of the Yoruba tribe.

The music Estefan presented in *Mi Tierra*

called to mind the "good old days" of the heyday of Havana nightclubs. The era could also be called "the bad old days," of course, before Castro came to power, since at that time Cuban nightlife was a corrupt affair. Organized crime from the United States controlled it. But the music of *Mi Tierra* was Gloria's sentimental voyage into the Cuban past. Cubans missed their homeland and respected their musical and cultural heritage. The song

Estefan's 1993 Spanish-language album, Mi Tierra, *was inspired by the music of legendary Cuban performers, such as the members of the Buena Vista Social Club, shown here in a 1998 concert at New York's Carnegie Hall.*

"Mi Tierra" is the lament of a man who missed the country of his birth. Sung by a Cuban, it amounted to a political statement, a cry for attention from a refugee.

At a press event to publicize the release, Gloria dressed in a revealing gown and wore orchids at the low neckline and in her hair. Her image evoked the sensual atmosphere of old Cuba's nightlife. Nobody dressed that way in the new Cuba, where Castro always wore military clothing.

Sales and reviews of the album were excellent. And Estefan finally won a Grammy—for the Best Tropical Latin Album of 1993—at the awards ceremony on March 1, 1994. Emilio had another cause for jubilation. Perhaps looking forward to a time when Gloria would no longer choose to sing and tour, or perhaps simply spurred on by his own restless energy, Emilio began grooming another Cuban refugee, Jon Secada, who had worked as a backup singer for Gloria with the Miami Sound Machine. Emilio produced Secada's album *Otro Día Más Sin Verte* (which translates as "just another day"). It went to the top of the *Billboard* magazine charts in the Latin music category in February 1993 and won a Grammy for Best Latin Pop album for 1992.

Gloria made two more albums quickly, *Christmas Through Your Eyes* in 1993 and *Hold Me, Thrill Me, Kiss Me* in 1994. Combined sales of

Emilio Estefan protégé Jon Secada, also a Cuban refugee, poses here with his 1993 Grammy award for Best Latin Pop Album.

these three albums went way over the multimillion mark during the next few years. She also had her name and star added to the Walk of Fame in Hollywood and received an honorary doctorate in music from the University of Miami. And she was honored for her contributions as an artist and entertainer by the Coalition of Hispanic American Women.

So Gloria had recovered from her accident, put out more reflective albums with songs about triumph over adversity, and returned to explore her childhood roots. Now it was time for her to face another challenge. She turned her attention to her dream of having a second child. But after some time trying, she discovered she couldn't become pregnant again, and she didn't know why. After several tests, a doctor told her that one of her fallopian tubes had been damaged in the terrible highway accident. Again she was lucky. The tube, which carries the egg down to meet the sperm, was repairable.

In spring 1994, Estefan became pregnant again, and in December she gave birth to a daughter, Emily Marie. This time Gloria didn't have to throw herself full force into touring. Her career was on solid ground. She stayed home to take care of her daughter and work on her music. At the time, her son Nayib was about ready to graduate from the eighth grade. Gloria discovered he was

Estefan poses with daughter Emily Marie.

musical, too. He played in his school band and had a drum set in his room.

At this time she gave an interviewer a peek into her heart and concerns as a celebrity and a parent. In an April 1994 interview for *USA Weekend,* Estefan expressed her thoughts on the Michael Jackson scandal, in which the superstar was accused of child molestation. She said it was a horror story for a celebrity. "If he's innocent . . . and they've been able to do this to his life, it's a horrendous thing. That was very scary, because it could just be a false accusation, and anyone can go into your stuff. You get tried in the media before anything ever happens. If he's guilty, I feel bad for children, because they don't have any heroes to look up to. Here's the supreme children's hero. That's a blow to kids."

Gloria said she talked about some things like that with her son. She didn't want him to sleep at other people's houses, and at the same time she didn't want him to have an abnormal life. "You have to explain things that can happen. Under no circumstances would I let my child sleep over with a man. I don't care how childlike that man is. [Jackson] probably didn't have a childhood. Because, let me tell you, (touring is) a big responsibility, even as an adult." She also claimed that she didn't like to watch herself on television. "I was already there. It's like working again, like reliving the whole experience. I let Emilio watch it."[4]

While at home with her family, she worked on material for an album to be called *Abriendo Puertas,* about opening doors, that she hoped would be a follow-up to her great success with *Mi Tierra.* The new album contained a mixture of music from many Latin American countries. She explained, in a video called *Everlasting Gloria!,* that this music supported her philosophy that people should move forward, never dwell on past troubles, and try to heal old wounds. Also, she wanted the public to gain an understanding of the Hispanic culture, with its love of music and dancing at social gatherings.

> **She told several writers that she had an American head and a Cuban heart.**

Once again, the National Academy of Recording Artists and Sciences recognized the quality of her work and awarded Estefan another Grammy. This time it was for Best Tropical Latin Performance. With two Grammys, the highest awards the music industry can bestow upon its artists, Estefan had proof that she was both an American and Cuban success story. She told several writers that she had an American head and a Cuban heart.

In early 1995, Estefan agreed to entertain Cuban refugees detained at Guantanamo, the tiny American military base that the U.S. maintained on Cuba. The base was a thorn in the side of Fidel Castro. The refugees were destined to be permitted by U.S. law to find a safe haven in the United States. Gloria performed for them on a stage with the Caribbean Sea as her backdrop; she sang her hits—among them "Rhythm Is Gonna Get You," "Can't Stay Away From You," and songs from *Mi Tierra*—and of course her wildly exciting "Conga." This brought American troops and Cuban refugees waiting for legal papers to their feet to form a conga line and dance together.

By the end of the year, Nayib Estefan, then a student at Gulliver Prep School, was working semiprofessionally as a drummer in a band called Psychosis. The group was preparing its first CD for release. In December 1995, the *Miami Herald's* Youth Only section published an interview with the fledgling musician, nicknamed Joey. All he wanted for Christmas was a new drum set. "If you could have anything you wanted right now, what would it be?" the interviewer asked. "I'd want my band to be famous . . . ," he said. He saw his future as "a movie director or the drummer in a band." Nayib had begun playing drums "with the drummer of my mother's band when she was on tour. Then I started playing on my own." His most embarrassing moment was when a drumstick flew out of his hand when he was performing in front of an audience. "I thought fast and found another one," he said.

"Do your parents like the music you play?" the writer asked. Nayib (Joey) answered, "Yes, they're very supportive of my band and very proud of me."[5]

CHAPTER SIX

CELEBRATING VICTORIES

In 1995, their adopted "hometown" of Miami Beach, the Estefans were spending an afternoon on their motorboat, the *Intrepid,* on Biscayne Bay. They headed out to sea for a while, then decided to go back to their dock at Star Island. On the way home, they encountered a jet-powered boat carrying two tourists from the North. Some boaters like to try to jump over the wakes of other boats. They considered it a great sport. The waves of a boat's wake can make another boat bounce up and down. It seemed to the Estefans that the tourists had that game in mind.

The driver, a young man, was approaching on the left of the Estefan boat. It will never be determined if he was trying to jump the wake of the Estefans' boat or if he simply lost control. But his boat turned sharply and hit the much larger *Intrepid.* The accident knocked the driver and his girlfriend out of their boat. The girl fell away from the boats and escaped injury. But the young man got cut very badly by the propeller blades of the Estefans' boat. Emilio jumped in the water, despite the threat of sharks being attracted to the blood, and pulled the victim to safety while Gloria telephoned for medical help. But it was too late. The victim, a young law student, died.

Gloria was terribly upset. Emilio was immediately tested for drinking alcohol, but all he had drunk that day was bottled water. It seemed that the dead man had probably been very inexperienced in handling his boat. In response, Gloria Estefan rose to the task of trying to prevent other such accidents. Florida had about three times as many boating accidents as any other state in the nation. Watersports are a big attraction in Florida, so politicians there didn't want to pass laws to control the watersports industry. They didn't want to do anything to discourage tourists or dampen their high spirits. But Estefan decided that she would lobby for training requirements and licenses for young, inexperienced drivers. She felt that Florida had to try to turn the tide against brutal, needless accidents.

In the state capital of Tallahassee, at the State House, the tiny, dark-haired singer and her entourage, including Emilio, were greeted by reporters at a hearing on legislation for ways to

Estefan testifies before the Florida state senate to encourage the passage of stricter boating laws. Earlier that year, the Estefans were involved in a deadly accident with an inexperienced boater.

improve water safety. Florida Representative James King Jr. later said, "The hackles on my neck went up" at the sight of her. King had been fighting controls on boating for many years. He didn't want to damage the economy of the boating industry. But other legislators had put forward some legislation to institute boating education and cut down on the deaths and injuries that marred the water sports industry in Florida. Gloria immediately got the crowd on her side by saying, "I came here as a citizen of Miami Beach, a citizen of the state of Florida, and obviously the celebrity has a little bit to do with why I am here."[1] Both she and the audience laughed.

She went on to say she had been boating for many years and had taken courses in navigation, seamanship, and piloting to make her hobby safe. She explained how simple incidents had led to tragic, fatal accidents. When seaweed gets stuck in a boat's intake pipe, the boat stalls. When a novice lets go of the choke, the driver doesn't get more control just because the boat slows down. The driver actually loses control over steering. Representative King and Gloria debated for a while. He actually became tongue-tied, but Gloria had stage presence from all her years as an entertainer. And she was morally committed to her task. At last, the representative said he thought this was the year that a boating safety law should go into effect. The law was passed in both the senate and the house in Florida. The bill went into effect in May 1996. Anyone operating an engine of ten horsepower or more now has to take boating education courses, and youngsters needed identification cards.[2]

The next year, the *Miami Herald* reported that Florida had a big drop in the number of boating deaths—though a few counties, including Dade, where the Estefans live, still had a big problem with accidents. But because of the new awareness and legislation Gloria helped pass, the number of people taking boating safety courses jumped from four thousand to twenty thousand.

Gloria's work on behalf of others continued to earn her positive attention from writers.

Gloria's work on behalf of others continued to earn her positive attention from writers. In person, they found her charming and down-to-earth, with a bright-eyed, intelligent, expressive face. Celebrity interviewer James Brady, writing about her in *Parade* magazine, said, "She may be the most popular entertainer in this hemisphere and has been called the most positive role model in the music business. And when Gloria Estefan talks about the shattering bus crash that broke her back, her sincerity is such that even the usual healthy skepticism of the reporter is suspended."

She told Brady, "If you could somehow get this across, that I couldn't have gotten through all this without good wishes and prayers . . . and it didn't matter to whom the prayers were offered. . . . I felt people's prayers. Unconditional love is so important to get you through the pain and fear."

She also expressed her allegiances. "Miami is my town. America is my country. But Cuba is *mi tierra* (my homeland)." Brady wrote, "Her crossover music is like that—madly popular with the Spanish-speaking but also popular with English-speaking Americans and Europeans."[3]

Her interviews with writers, whether for print or television, tended to be inspirational. She was fond of saying that she never liked to dwell on the terrible problems that could arise in life. She liked to leave them behind and go forward. That was the most important thing. Moving forward. Doing one's best. She also had great humor and honesty, not only about her career and the life-and-death problems she had faced, but also about the smaller ones of her day-to-day life as a wife and mother. Success has not spoiled her. Leonard Pitts Jr., pop music critic for the *Miami Herald,* once noted how fans kept interrupting her meal at a Miami restaurant one day. Pitts wrote: "Gloria handled each one with unfailing grace. She nodded, she chatted, and, I'm sure, made each of those people feel like the center of her universe for those few moments." Pitts compared her behavior with that of some other pop stars he had observed. They kept people waiting at performances and snarled at fans who tried to approach them.[4] Estefan, however, had built a reputation for being pleasant and approachable from the earliest days of her career.

Regarding her family, Estefan told a *Ladies Home Journal* writer that she had never expected to love anyone as much as she adored Nayib, and then along came her daughter Emily. Nayib had inspired her to write "Nayib's Song" for the album, *Into the Light*. Emily inspired Gloria to compose "Along Came You." She also told of some of the antics engaged in by her son, "who recently got expelled from his exclusive prep school after making a crank call to a classmate's mother, impersonating a school official and telling the woman that her son was being suspended for throwing food in the cafeteria." As punishment, Gloria made her son work with the construction crew building a guest house for the Estefan family on Star Island. "He had to get up early, use the jackhammer and everything, the same shift as everyone else. No favors," Gloria said.

She called Nayib "a gigantic ham. He's pulled a lot of pranks. But what do you expect when his forty-three year old father hides around the house and jumps out to scare the housekeeper, or makes crank calls to my mother, pretending to be someone from the press?" Gloria rolled her eyes.[5] She thought the work she forced Nayib to do would teach him an important lesson.

She told writer James Brady that she didn't think a parent could ever spoil children by giving them too much love. But on the other hand, it was clear that she didn't want her kids getting away with too much mischief. When she had been a child with hard luck as her daily portion, life—and survival—had always been serious for her. "My life was home and school," she told Leonard Pitts Jr. "That was it. I felt very old. I felt mature and responsible."[6] She had never lost her sense of humor. But she tried to keep her values—and her son's—in good order to prepare him to deal with the realities of life. They could be hard, she knew.

In the 1990s, too, Emilio promoted yet another singer, a Cuban pop star, Albita Rodríguez, who recorded for Emilio's Crescent Moon label, named for his recording studio. The Estefans also bought the Cardozo Hotel in the trendy South Beach area of Miami Beach, among other properties, and then opened a restaurant at Disney World. They donated money to a variety of charities, including the New World Symphony, a symphony orchestra with facilities for training gifted students. Gloria often gave money to charities through the United Way. And Estefan funds went to organizations that fought cancer and searched for stranded refugees and rafters in the Florida Straits. Cyn Zarco, writing for *USA Weekend,* mentioned to her that in Miami she was treated like a saint. Gloria replied. "It's ridiculous. I'm just a normal person. I love to do good things. . . . But I'm certainly no saint."[7] And to Leonard Pitts Jr. she said with a laugh, "I'm going to have to do something evil to get rid of this goody image. It's funny to me. I'm no saint. I'm a normal human being. I love doing good things. I think we all should. But there's a little devil in all of us."

In 1996, Estefan again achieved fame when her inspirational song "Reach" was adopted by the Atlanta Summer Olympic Games organizers. The tune, which was taken from the album *Destiny,* focused on the need to try one's best and featured an emotionally stirring march rhythm at the end. It earned Estefan a nomination for a Grammy for Best Female Pop Vocal Performance. Although the song didn't win, it helped uplift and soothe the spirits of people after the deadly bombing in Atlanta's Centennial Park. Gloria's performance there was part of her "Evolution World Tour," as she called it, which took her to many American cities and foreign countries and ended in late September with a series of concerts in Miami. At the Miami performances, she included her son and daughter, with Nayib taking little Emily by the hand and walking onstage. The crowd was touched by the charming family scene.

Estefan, who turned forty-one years old on September 1, 1998, took part in many television shows, spectacles, and special events in the late 1990s. She sang a duet with Frank Sinatra on his album of collaborations with other singers. She also sang on an all-star album, "Dave Grusin Presents West Side Story," on the N2K label in 1998. That year, too, she appeared onstage with the great Aretha Franklin in a VH1 concert featuring several pop divas. Like all the other singers in that concert, Gloria was outdone by the powerful soul singer Franklin, according to the critics. (But that was to be expected. No singer ever outdid Aretha.) Estefan also sang in a televised tribute in honor of soul singer Ray Charles' fiftieth anniversary in show business. And she appeared at Radio City Music Hall for the thirtieth-anniversary, all-star musical tribute to *Sesame Street,* performing alongside the Muppets, comedian Rosie O'Donnell, and many others. Estefan also released a new album, called *Gloria!* By June 1998, only her name was really needed for a title. Or it might have been enough just to feature her picture with an exclamation point!

Such things occupied her time in public. But

Estefan performs with Celine Dion (left) and Shania Twain (right) on the VH1 Divas! concert.

she wasn't rushing around the world all the time anymore. The Estefans had millions of dollars in the bank and in investments. Nobody knew for sure how much, because the Estefan family fortune is held privately. And Emilio Estefan keeps details of his business affairs very quiet—even secret. Emilio and Gloria Estefan are president and vice president, respectively, of their business organization, and they share in their ventures equally.[8]

Even though Estefan didn't really need to earn more money, and she had enough fame to last her for a lifetime, she kept working. She served as a guest host on The Rosie O'Donnell Show, and she acted in a film, *The Music of My Heart,* shot in New York City, with Meryl Streep in 1998. Gloria became the honorary chairperson for a volunteer project called Kidzcare, which was created to help families and kids with HIV and AIDS. And in 1999, she recorded a Spanish-language album. Finally, Estefan starred in her own New Year's Eve stage show, *The Gloria Estefan Millennium Concert Spectacular,* at Miami's new

Estefan sings at the launch party for her Gloria! *album at New York's legendary Studio 54.*

American Airlines Arena. The tireless Emilio Estefan was working on the developing ideas of television shows and movies in connection with a company called Universal Television.

Of her lifestyle at the end of the twentieth century, Estefan said, "I'm very happy to have my career because I'm doing what I truly love to do. Music and singing were always very much a part of me, and being able to do it all the time is more than I ever hoped for. I just hope that I can grow in my career, continue writing, and hopefully still be around a while."[9]

Gloria said she had been given the privilege to be creative in her life.

In part, because of her strength of character and her determination, her dream seemed to be a prophecy. Life continued to go smoothly for the Estefans. She was "in a very celebratory part" of her life, as she said to an interviewer in the 1995 video, *Everlasting Gloria!* in 1995, sitting in a palatial room in her palatial house on Star Island. Gloria said she had been given the privilege to be creative in her life. She had the baby daughter that she had wanted so much. Her son was approaching adulthood. "If things would just stay like this, that would be great," she said. And so far, they have.

The late 1990s were very busy for Gloria Estefan,
shown here in a quiet moment with her pet wallabies.

NOTES

CHAPTER ONE

1. Associated Press, March 20, 1990.
2. Lisa Robinson, "Glory, Gloria Hallelujah," *New York Post,* Friday, Feb. 25, 1994.
3. Gloria Estefan as told to Kathryn Casey, "My Miracle," *Ladies Home Journal,* August, 1990.
4. Ibid.
5. Anthony M. DeStefano, *Gloria Estefan, The Pop Superstar From Tragedy to Triumph,* New York: Signet Books, 1997.
6. Susan Heller Anderson, "Chronicle," *New York Times,* March 29, 1990.
7. Gloria Estefan as told to Kathryn Casey, "My Miracle," *Ladies Home Journal,* August, 1990.
8. Ibid.
9. Laura Morice, "Gloria Hallelujah!," *McCall's,* July, 1995, quoted in DeStefano.

CHAPTER TWO

1. "Gloria Estefan: An Intimate Portrait," Walker/Fitzgibbons Television & Film Productions in association with Estefan Enterprises, rebroadcast on Lifetime Television, January 6, 1997.
2. Christopher John Farley, "From a Cuban Heart," *Time,* July 8, 1996.
3. "Gloria Estefan," *Current Biography Yearbook,* 1995, 147–51.
4. Mary Beth McEvily, "Gloria Estefan: Making It Happen," *Shape,* March 1990.
5. "Gloria Estefan," *Current Biography Yearbook,* 1995, 147–51.
6. "Gloria Estefan: An Intimate Portrait."
7. "Gloria Estefan," *Current Biography Yearbook,* 1995, 147–51.
8. Ibid.

CHAPTER THREE

1. "Gloria Estefan: An Intimate Portrait," Walker/Fitzgibbons Television & Film Productions in association with Estefan Enterprises, rebroadcast on Lifetime Television, January 6, 1997.
2. Ibid.
3. Ibid.
4. Ibid.

5. Mary Beth McEvily, "Gloria Estefan: Making It Happen," *Shape,* March 1990. *People,* October 1986.
6. John Rockwell, "Placido Domingo Sings A Finale to Arts Festival," *New York Times,* July 12, 1988.
7. Stephen Holden, "Salsa Spice From Miami," *New York Times,* July 29, 1988.
8. "Gloria Estefan," *Current Biography Yearbook,* 1995.

CHAPTER FOUR

1. Melina Gerosa, "Gloria's Greatest Hits," *Ladies' Home Journal,* August 1996.
2. Anthony M. DeStefano, *Gloria Estefan, The Pop Superstar From Tragedy to Triumph,* New York: Signet Books, 1997.
3. Ibid.
4. Juan Carlos Coto, "Estefan's Comeback Concert," *Miami Herald,* March 2, 1991.
5. DeStefano.
6. Ibid.
7. Mary Beth McEvily, "Gloria Estefan: Making It Happen," *Shape,* March 1990.
8. Fernando Gonzalez, "Emilio Estefan Has Vision of Motown With Latin Beat," *Miami Herald,* January 17, 1994.

CHAPTER FIVE

1. Anthony M. DeStefano, *Gloria Estefan, The Pop Superstar From Tragedy to Triumph,* New York: Signet Books, 1997.
2. Carol Pugh, "Gloria Estefan Keeps Her Music Free of Politics," *Miami Herald,* February 2, 1992.
3. Leonard Pitts Jr., "Gloria Goes Back to Her Roots," *Miami Herald,* June 22, 1993.
4. Cyn Zarco, "Gloria Estefan Stops the Music," *USA Weekend,* April, 1–3, 1994.
5. Lizabeth Redman, "The Other Estefan," *Miami Herald,* December 20, 1995.

CHAPTER SIX

1. Anthony M. DeStefano, *Gloria Estefan, The Pop Superstar From Tragedy to Triumph,* New York: Signet Books, 1997.
2. Ibid.
3. James Brady, "In Step With Gloria Estefan," *Parade,* April 28, 1996.
4. Leonard Pitts, Jr., "Why Do Fans Keep Cheering Performers with Attitudes?," *Miami Herald,* July 14, 1993.
5. Melina Gerosa, "Gloria's Greatest Hits," *Ladies Home Journal,* August, 1994.

6. Leonard Pitts, Jr., "Gloria Goes Back to Her Roots," *Miami Herald,* June 22, 1993.
7. Cyn Zarco, "Gloria Estefan Stops the Music," *USA Weekend,* April, 1–3, 1994.
8. Destefano.
9. Mary Beth McEvily, "Gloria Estefan: Making It Happen," *Shape,* March 1990.

CHRONOLOGY

Sept. 1, 1957	Gloria María Fajardo is born in Havana, Cuba, to Gloria and José Manuel Fajardo.
1959	The Fajardos escape to Miami, Florida, after the Cuban Revolution.
1961	Manuel Fajardo returns to Cuba as a U.S. soldier during the Bay of Pigs invasion. He is captured and imprisoned for a year and a half.
1962	Fajardo is freed and returns home. Gloria begins her interest in music as a refuge.
1964	Rebecca Fajardo is born
1966	Manuel Fajardo leaves for a tour of duty in the Vietnam War. Gloria receives a guitar from her mother and teaches herself to play.
1968	Gloria's father returns home and quickly sickens.

	Gloria's mother finds work as a teacher, and Gloria takes over care of her father.
1973	Manuel Fajardo's condition worsens and he is moved to a veteran's administration hospital.
1974	Gloria and cousin Mercedes begin singing together at weekend parties.
1975	Gloria enters the University of Miami on a partial scholarship.
	She meets fellow Cuban refugee Emilio Estefan, who convinces her and Mercedes to sing with his group, the Miami Rhythm Boys.
1976	Emilio and Gloria become engaged on the night of the Bicentennial celebration.
1977	The Miami Rhythm Boys makes its first self-produced recording.
Sept. 2, 1978	Emilio and Gloria marry.
1978	The group makes a second recording.
1979	The group makes a third recording.
	At the suggestion of a producer, Emilio changes the group's name to The Miami Sound Machine.
1980	Nayib Estefan is born.
	The Miami Sound Machine signs a contract with CBS Discos Distribution and tours Central and South America.
Mid-1980s	Miami Sound Machine recordings top the charts in Latin America.

The group releases "Dr. Beat," its first crossover hit.

The group releases *Eyes of Innocence,* its first English-language recording.

The group releases *Primitive Love,* its second English-language album. The single "Conga" becomes a hit, topping for music categories.

Internal struggles within the band result in some members' departure.

1987   The band is renamed Gloria Estefan and the Miami Sound Machine.

The band releases its third album, *Let It Loose.* Four songs reach the top ten on the pop charts.

The band performs at the World Series in St. Louis.

1988   Estefan performs at the first New York International Festival of the Arts in Central Park. Estefan sings a duet with opera star Placido Domingo.

The Estefans build a multimillion-dollar home on Miami Beach's exclusive Star Island.

1990   March 20: Estefan's back is broken after her tour bus is rear-ended by a tractor trailer outside Scranton, Pennsylvania.

1991   January: Estefan makes her first public appearance after the accident. She performs on the American Music Awards.

Estefan releases *Into the Light,* which features the hit single "Coming Out of the Dark."

March: Estefan performs at the opening of the Miami Arena.

June: Estefan performs at the White House for President George Bush.

1992   Estefan performs at a relief concert for victims of Hurricane Andrew in Florida. She receives the Humanitarian of the Year Award from B'nai B'rith, a group devoted to fighting discrimination.

She wins the Alexis de Tocqueville Award from the United Way of Dade County, Florida, for her volunteer work. Estefan is appointed honorary delegate to the United Nations by George Bush.

1993   Estefan releases *Mi Tierra,* an album of songs harkening back to pre-Castro Cuba.

Estefan wins her first Grammy Award, for Best Tropical Latin Album.

Estefan releases *Christmas Through Your Eyes.*

1994   Estefan releases *Hold Me, Thrill Me, Kiss Me.*

Her name and star are added to the Hollywood Walk of Fame.

She receives an honorary doctorate from the University of Miami.

Estefan is honored by the Coalition of Hispanic American Women.

Emily Marie Estefan is born.

1995   Estefan releases *Abriendo Puertas*, which wins Estefan a second Grammy.

Estefan entertains Cuban refugees at Guantánamo, the tiny American military base on Cuba.

1996   The Estefans are involved (the previous year) in a boating accident in which a man is killed. As a result, Estefan testifies before the Florida state legislature in favor of stricter boating regulations after discovering the man was not trained in boating safety.

Estefan's song "Reach," from the album *Destiny,* is adopted by the Summer Olympic Games in Atlanta as its theme. She performs the song in Atlanta's Centennial Park after the bombing there.

Estefan is nominated for the Best Female Pop Vocal Performance Grammy. She does not win.

1998   Estefan performs on an album of duets with Frank Sinatra and on an all-star album entitled *Dave Grusin Presents West Side Story.*

Estefan appears on the VH1 Divas special and on a tribute to Ray Charles.

Estefan appears in the 30th-anniverstary tribute to Sesame Street at New York's Radio City Music Hall.

Estefan releases the album *Gloria!* and performs at the Superbowl.

1999   Estefan appears in the film *Music of the Heart,* starring actress Meryl Streep.

Estefan serves as guest host of *The Rosie O'Donnell Show.*

Estefan records another Spanish-language album.

Estefan stars in her own New Year's Eve show at Miami's new American Airlines Arena.

DISCOGRAPHY

Eyes of Innocence, Miami Sound Machine, Epic Records, a division of CBS Records, Inc., 1984. Contains the hit "Dr. Beat."

Primitive Love, Miami Sound Machine, Epic, 1985. Contains the hit "Conga."

Let It Loose, Gloria Estefan and the Miami Sound Machine, Epic, 1987. Contains the hit "Rhythm Is Gonna Get You."

Cuts Both Ways, Gloria Estefan, Epic, 1989. Contains the song "Oye Mi Canto" in both English and Spanish.

Into the Light, Gloria Estefan, Epic, 1991. Contains the song "Coming Out of the Dark."

Destiny, Gloria Estefan, Epic, 1996. Contains the song "Reach," which became very popular after Estefan sang it at the Olympic Games in Atlanta, Georgia.

Gloria! Gloria Estefan, Epic, 1998.

Gloria Estefan has also appeared as a guest singer or backing vocalist on albums with other performers, such as singer Frank Sinatra and pianist Dave Grusin.

VIDEOGRAPHY

Primitive Love, Epic, 1985.
Let It Loose, Epic, 1987.
Cuts Both Ways, Epic, 1989.
Evolution, CBS Music Video Enterprises, 1990.
Coming Out of the Dark, Sony Music Video Enterprises, 1991.
Into The Light, Epic, 1991.
Into the Light, World Tour, 1991, Sony Music Video Enterprises, 1992.
Greatest Hits, Epic, 1992.
Mi Tierra, Epic, 1993.
Hold Me, Thrill Me, Kiss Me, Epic, 1994.
Abrienda Puertas, Epic, 1995.
Everlasting Gloria!, Epic Music Video, 1995.
Destiny, Epic, 1996.

This is only a sampling of the material available. Some titles are also available on laser disk.

FOR MORE INFORMATION

Boulais, Sue. *Gloria Estefan*. Childs, MD.: Mitchell Lane, 1998.

Delisi, Jeanette. *Gloria Estefan: Destiny*. Miami, FL.: Warner Bros., 1996.

———. *Gloria Estefan: Mi Tierra*. Warner Bros., 1993.

DeStefano, Anthony M. *Gloria Estefan*. New York: Signet Books, 1997.

Gonzalez, Fernando. *Gloria Estefan: Cuban American Singing Star*, New York: Millbrook Press, 1993.

Nielson, Shelly. *Gloria Estefan, International Pop Star*. Minneapolis, MN.: Abdo and Daughters, 1993.

Rodriguez, Janel. *Gloria Estefan*. Chatham, NJ: Raintree Steck-Vaughan, 1996.

Shirley, David. *Gloria Estefan: Queen of Latin Pop*. New York: Chelsea House, 1994.

Stefoff, Rebecca. *Gloria Estefan*. New York: Chelsea House, 1991.

Strazzabosco, Jeanne M. *Learning About Determination From The Life of Gloria Estefan*. New York: Rosen, 1996.

INDEX

▲ 110 ▲

ABOUT THE AUTHOR

Leslie Gourse has researched and written stories for various media, including CBS and the *New York Times.* Her articles and stories have appeared in magazines and newspapers, covering general culture, social trends, and music. Her books, including *Dizzy Gillespie and the Birth of Bebop,* and *Blowing on the Changes: The Art of the Jazz Horn Players,* have earned high praise from the critics.